CHRIS EVANS
Making a Difference as an Actor

By Katie Kawa

People Who Make a Difference

KidHaven
PUBLISHING

Published in 2023 by
KidHaven Publishing, an Imprint of Greenhaven Publishing, LLC
29 E. 21st Street
New York, NY 10010

Designer: Deanna Paternostro
Editor: Katie Kawa

Photo credits: Cover, pp. 15, 17 Featureflash Photo Agency/Shutterstock.com; p. 5 BAKOUNINE/Shutterstock.com; p. 7 s_bukley/Shutterstock.com; p. 9 MRP/Alamy Stock Photo; p. 11 PA Images/Alamy Stock Photo; pp. 13, 20 Tinseltown/Shutterstock.com; p. 18 Jaguar PS/Shutterstock.com; p. 21 T.Sumaetho/Shutterstock.com.

Cataloging-in-Publication Data

Names: Kawa, Katie.
Title: Chris Evans: making a difference as an actor / Katie Kawa.
Description: New York : KidHaven Publishing, 2023. | Series: People who make a difference | Includes glossary and index.
Identifiers: ISBN 9781534541696(pbk.) | ISBN 9781534541719 (library bound) | ISBN 9781534541702 (6pack) | ISBN 9781534541726 (ebook)
Subjects: LCSH: Evans, Chris, 1981—Juvenile literature. | Actors–United States–Biography–Juvenile literature.
Classification: LCC PN2287.E77 K39 2023 | DDC 791.4302'8092 B–dc23

Printed in the United States of America

CPSIA compliance information: Batch #CSKH23: For further information contact Greenhaven Publishing LLC, New York, New York at 1-844-317-7404.

CONTENTS

"A GOOD MAN"

Chris Evans is best known for playing a superhero on the big screen. In the **Marvel Cinematic Universe** (MCU), he played Steve Rogers—also known as Captain America. In the movie *Captain America: The First Avenger*, this hero is described as "not a perfect soldier, but a good man."

"A good man" is a way many people have described Chris Evans too. He uses his voice to speak out about causes that matter to him. He also gives his time and money to help kids who are sick. These things and many more help make Chris Evans a real-life hero!

In His Words

"It's so important to … help shape the world we want to see."

— Tweet from June 2021

In the MCU, Captain America uses his super strength to make a difference. In the real world, Chris Evans uses his own strengths—including his honesty and his kindness—to make a difference too!

A BOSTON BOY

Chris's hometown is very important to him. He was born on June 13, 1981, in Boston, Massachusetts. He grew up in the town of Sudbury, which is close to the big city of Boston. Even today, Chris likes to go home to Boston to spend time with his family and childhood friends.

Family has always meant a lot to Chris. While he was growing up, his dad was a dentist, and his mother worked for a local youth theater. Chris has one brother, Scott, and two sisters, Carly and Shanna. **Performing** was a big part of life for the kids in the Evans family.

In His Words

"I was never much of a 'I can't wait to leave this town' kind of kid."

— Interview with *Men's Journal* magazine from April 2019

Chris is still very close with his family. He's shown here with his mother, Lisa, and his brother, Scott, who's also an actor.

GETTING HIS START

Chris started acting in school plays and **musicals** when he was a kid. He enjoyed being onstage and even went to acting camp. Chris's love for acting only got stronger as he got older. Before his last year of high school, he went to New York City to take classes at a famous acting school. He also worked for a casting company—a company that finds actors for different roles, or parts.

Chris finished high school early and continued acting. He had some small parts on TV shows and started getting work in movies. However, his big break was still to come.

In His Words

"I just liked acting. I have a soft spot for theater, because it was such a big part of my childhood, a very sweet chapter in my life."

— Interview with *Esquire* magazine from April 2020

Many other famous actors went to the same acting school as Chris—the Lee Strasberg Theatre & Film Institute. One of them is Scarlett Johansson, who has acted with Chris in many movies, including in the MCU.

EARLY SUPERHERO SUCCESS

Chris played parts in **comedies** before getting his first big part in an action movie in *Cellular*. This movie came out in 2004 and was about a man who has to help a woman who calls his cell phone after she's been kidnapped.

Chris also played a different superhero before be became Captain America. In 2005, he starred as Johnny Storm—also known as the Human Torch—in *Fantastic Four*. He played the same part again in *Fantastic 4: Rise of the Silver Surfer*, which came out in 2007. This was just a preview of the superhero superstardom waiting for Chris a few years later.

In His Words

"Maybe the thing you're most scared of is exactly what you should do."

— Interview with Motivation Madness YouTube channel from August 2017

The *Fantastic Four* movies helped show that Chris could play a superhero. They came out before the MCU made superhero movies as popular as they are today. Chris is shown here with the actors who played the other members of the Fantastic Four.

LIFE AS AN AVENGER

In 2011, people saw Chris as a superhero on the big screen once again. This time, though, he was starring in *Captain America: The First Avenger*. Chris also played Captain America in *The Avengers* in 2012, *Captain America: The Winter Soldier* in 2014, *Avengers: Age of Ultron* in 2015, and *Captain America: Civil War* in 2016. He appeared in *Spider-Man: Homecoming* in 2017 too.

Chris's last two appearances as Captain America were in *Avengers: Infinity War* in 2018 and *Avengers: Endgame* in 2019. He helped make the MCU a huge success, and Captain America became many kids' favorite superhero.

In His Words

"Cap is the steady hand on the wheel ... When you're playing a character for a long time ... You start to look at your own conflicts [problems] ... through the eyes of someone who might handle it better than you would."

— Interview with *Men's Journal* magazine from April 2019

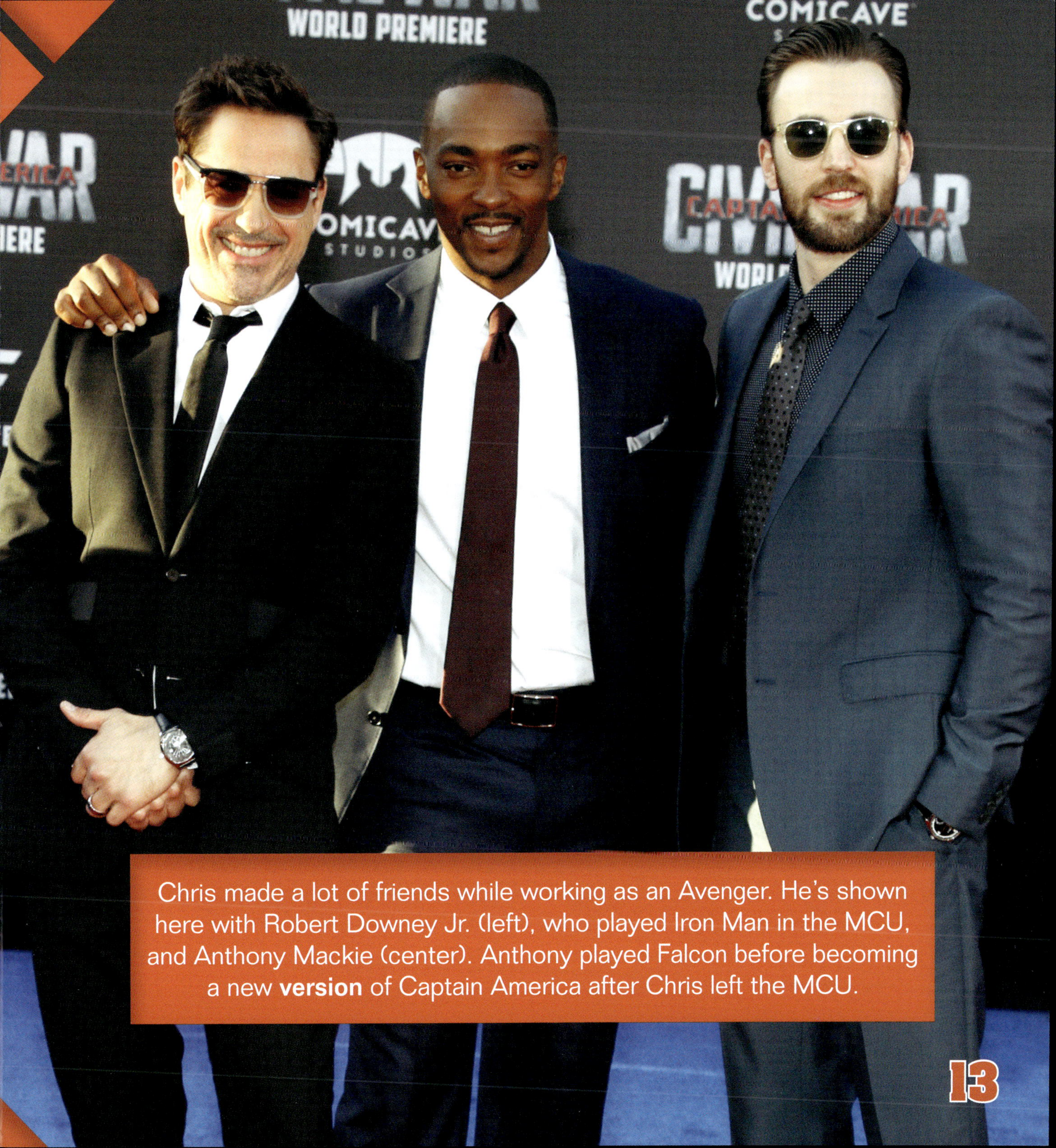

Chris made a lot of friends while working as an Avenger. He's shown here with Robert Downey Jr. (left), who played Iron Man in the MCU, and Anthony Mackie (center). Anthony played Falcon before becoming a new **version** of Captain America after Chris left the MCU.

PLAYING OTHER PARTS

When Chris wasn't playing Captain America, he was staying busy acting in other movies, such as *Gifted* in 2017. He also directed the 2014 movie *Before We Go* and has said he would love to direct more movies in the future.

After his time in the MCU was done, Chris still worked hard. He played the part of Ransom Drysdale in the popular movie *Knives Out* in 2019. He was also the voice of Buzz Lightyear in the **animated** movie *Lightyear,* which came out in June 2022. Chris loves animated movies, so being a part of one was a dream come true for him.

In His Words

"Animated movie were an enormous [huge] part of my childhood. They were my escape. My adventures. My dreams. They were my first window into the magic of storytelling and performing."

— Tweet from October 2021

Chris Evans became famous for playing a superhero, but he's starred in many other kinds of movies—from love stories and comedies to mysteries and animated adventures! He's shown here with some of the other actors from *Knives Out*.

A HERO WHO HELPS KIDS

One of the reasons Chris was excited to make *Lightyear* was because making kids happy means a lot to him. He wants to make a difference in the lives of young people, especially kids who are sick. He's visited kids in hospitals in Boston. He also visited a children's hospital in Seattle, Washington, with Chris Pratt, who plays Star-Lord in the MCU.

One of the **organizations** closest to Chris's heart is called Christopher's Haven. It provides families with places to live when kids are being treated for **cancer** in hospitals far from home. Chris has raised a lot of money over the years for Christopher's Haven.

In His Words

"Every time I speak with you guys [young people], I feel so **inspired**."

— Video chat with students from October 2020

Chris sometimes works with his fellow MCU actors to make a difference. In 2020, he raised money for groups that feed hungry families by giving people the chance to win a virtual, or online, game night with him and some of the other members of the MCU.

SPEAKING HIS MIND

Many people think that heroes have to be tough or that heroes don't cry. However, Chris is changing that harmful way of thinking by talking openly about his feelings. He's even spoken about his struggles with **anxiety**. Chris has said that it's not a bad thing to cry and to talk honestly about your **mental** health. This honesty helps other people feel less alone when they're having hard times.

Chris is also honest when he talks about politics, or ideas about the government. He's called attention to problems he sees in the world and supports leaders he thinks can help fix those problems.

In His Words

"I went to **therapy** ... I do struggle with ... anxiety about certain things."

— Interview with Motivation Madness YouTube channel from August 2017

The Life of Chris Evans

1981
Chris Evans is born on June 13 in Boston, Massachusetts.

2004
Chris acts in the movie *Cellular*.

2005
Chris plays Johnny Storm in *Fantastic Four*.

2007
Chris stars in *Fantastic 4: Rise of the Sliver Surfer*.

2011
Chris plays Captain America for the first time in *Captain America: The First Avenger*.

2012
The Avengers comes out.

2014
Chris stars in *Captain America: The Winter Soldier* and directs and acts in *Before We Go*.

2015
Avengers: Age of Ultron comes out.

2016
Chris stars in *Captain America: Civil War*.

2017
Chris stars in *Gifted* and appears in *Spider-Man: Homecoming*.

2018
Avengers: Infinity War comes out.

2019
Chris stars in his last MCU movie, *Avengers: Endgame*, and acts in *Knives Out*.

2020
Chris helps create the political website A Starting Point.

2022
Lightyear comes out, with Chris as the voice of Buzz Lightyear.

Chris has become a big star, and he's always busy with new projects!

STANDING UP FOR WHAT'S RIGHT

Chris knows that his voice is powerful, and he's using it to help others. He's also giving others a chance to use their voices. For example, in 2020, he helped create a website called A Starting Point. It features videos with government leaders in which they talk about different issues. Chris hopes this website can help people become more informed, or educated, citizens.

Captain America stands up for what he believes is right, and so does Chris Evans. From helping sick kids to speaking out about politics, he's doing his part to make the world a better place.

In His Words

"I think everyone who chooses to stay out of politics (which is your right) should make a mental note of where they would draw the line and feel it necessary to get involved. Then ask yourself, is it possible that point already happened, but it happened too slowly to notice."

— Tweet from October 2019

Be Like Chris Evans!

Talk openly about your feelings, and tell other people it's OK to talk about their feelings too.

Talk to your parents or other trusted adults about politics, and read about important issues so you can form your own informed opinions.

Write letters to government leaders about problems you think they can fix.

Stand up for what you believe is right.

Raise money for causes you care about, especially organizations in your community that help kids.

If you're struggling with anxiety or other problems with your mental health, tell a trusted adult.

Cheer up your friends or family members when they're sick or in the hospital by visiting them. You can make them a present or a card too.

Even if you don't have super strength or super speed, you can still make a difference in the world around you, just like Chris Evans does!

GLOSSARY

animated: Made using a series of drawings, pictures, or computer-created images that are shown quickly one after another.

anxiety: A mental condition marked by strong feelings of fear or nervousness about what might happen.

cancer: A sometimes deadly sickness in which cells grow in a way they should not, often forming tumors, or growths, that harm the body.

comedy: A play, movie, book, or TV show that is meant to make people laugh.

inspired: Moved to do something great.

Marvel Cinematic Universe: The group of Marvel movies and TV shows that share many of the same characters and began with *Iron Man* in 2008.

mental: Relating to the mind.

musical: A movie or a play that tells a story with songs and often dancing.

organization: A group formed for a specific purpose.

perform: To entertain people by singing, acting, or doing some other activity that requires skill.

therapy: A method used to treat a mental or physical health problem.

version: A form of something that is different from the ones that came before it.

FOR MORE INFORMATION

WEBSITES

IMDb: Chris Evans

www.imdb.com/name/nm0262635

The Internet Movie Database has a list of all the movies Chris Evans has acted in, as well as facts about his life.

Marvel Movies

www.marvel.com/movies

The official Marvel website has facts about all the Marvel movies, including every one that Chris Evans was in.

BOOKS

Bray, Adam. *Marvel Studios 101: All Your Questions Answered*. New York, NY: DK Publishing, 2018.

Donatelli, Jen Jones. *Chris Evans*. North Mankato, MN: Captsone Press, 2017.

Grange, Emma. *Marvel We Are Super Heroes: All Special, All Different, All Powerful*. New York, NY: DK Children, 2020.

INDEX